A Jewish

The Jewish Gladiator

by Michael Rosen

illustrated by Simon Jacob

Oh, my uncle's wedding was so boring! Well, it wasn't exactly the *wedding* that was boring. It was the *speeches* afterwards. On and on and on they went. Someone said the bride was lovely. Then the best man said my uncle was a lucky man. Then someone thanked the best man.

The best man thanked the bridesmaids. The bridesmaids thanked the lady who put out the flowers, and so she thanked the lady who put out the vases that the flowers were in, and then that lady thanked another lady for fetching the vases that the flowers were in … on and on and on they went.

The next day, I was moaning about the boring speeches to my brother, when my dad said, "Well, a boring speech is not always such a bad thing."

"What do you mean?" I said.

"Let me tell you the story of the Jewish gladiator and you'll see what I mean," said Dad.

"Jewish gladiator? What was his name?" I said.

"Sammy."

"Sammy who?"

"Sammy Berkowitz," he said, and he settled down to tell us the story.

In Ancient Rome, there was nothing people liked better than to watch a gladiator fight. The gladiators were poor slaves, who might have to fight lions, bears, tigers or men in armour. If by some miracle they escaped with their lives, the gladiators would be set free.

One day, Sammy Berkowitz was called up to fight the lions.

Not the bears, the tigers or the men in armour – but the lions. Now, you know, not one gladiator who had faced the lions ever, ever, ever came out alive. Those Ancient Romans had big special hungry lions that spent day and night longing to gobble up a man. You could hear them in their cages roaring: "Ooooh, give me a man to eat! Rrrraaaaaahhh!"

Most of the gladiators, poor fellows, were scared stiff of the lions. “Not the lions, please, not the lions,” they would say to each other, trembling with fear.

But when Sammy Berkowitz heard that it was his turn to go out and face the lions, he didn't seem to be worried one little bit. He sat there, in the gladiators' cell, eating the bagel he had made earlier – filled with his favourite chopped herring – and tapping his feet.

A new gladiator, one who had come all the way from England, was puzzled by Sammy's lack of nerves.

"I say, old chap," he said to Sammy, "you not worried at all?"

"Worried? What is there to worry about?" said Sammy. "What is this life after all? You come in one end, you go out the other." In the cages just along the corridor you could hear the lions roaring. "Give me a juicy man to eat! Rrrraaaaaahhh!" Sammy shrugged his shoulders and took another bite of his bagel.

With a sudden crash, the big iron doors were thrown open. Two huge guards stomped into the cell, grabbed Sammy, and dragged him out, along the tunnel and into the stadium. More iron doors clanked shut behind him. Sammy stood alone, right in the middle of the great arena, under the hot sun.

How the crowd laughed. They were used to seeing massive warriors, men with bulging muscles, who would wrestle and fight bears, tigers and men in armour. But who was this? Someone who looked like he couldn't fight his way out of a paper bag.

And, what do you know? He actually *had* a paper bag in one hand, and his chopped herring bagel in the other!

The crowd laughed and clapped. This was going to be fun. Some huge lion would be sure to gobble him up in about two mouthfuls.

But Sammy still didn't seem to mind one little bit. He just stood there munching away.

The next moment, two more massive iron gates opened, there was a huge roar and out rushed a fierce lion. At last, some dinner! There in front of the lion was a juicy little man, Sammy Berkowitz. The lion bounded closer and closer to Sammy. But then, just as it was about to leap on him, Sammy raised his arm.

The lion stopped. Sammy leaned over and whispered in the lion's ear. At that, the lion turned round and walked slowly back to his cage.

The crowd booed and hissed. This wasn't what they had paid to see.

Up in his royal box, the Roman Emperor was furious. What had the lion-trainers been doing? Wasn't it their job to train their lions to be vicious, furious, raging beasts? "Send in another lion!" he yelled. "And make it a really scary one this time!"

So the guards opened up *another* gate and out rushed *another* lion, this one even fiercer than the one before. The crowd yelled and screamed. Surely this lion would rip Sammy Berkowitz apart and eat him up, every little bit?

This lion rushed across the stadium, baring his teeth and roaring.

And just as before, Sammy just stood there waiting, and just at the moment the lion was about to pounce on him, Sammy raised his arm, leaned over and whispered in the lion's ear. Immediately, the lion stopped in his tracks, turned tail and slunk back to his cage.

This time the crowd quite liked Sammy's trick. Some of them clapped.

But the Emperor was not pleased at all. "Send in The Lion Hercules!" he thundered.

Hercules? The name went all round the stadium. Not Hercules, surely?

Hercules was the fiercest lion ever known in Ancient Rome. He was famous for fighting ten armed men at once, killing them all and eating them, helmets and all. Surely not Hercules?

But Hercules it was. The cage doors opened and out rushed the great Hercules, his muscles bulging, his claws out, his giant teeth gleaming in the sun. With giant leaps, he bounded across the stadium towards Sammy.

But as before, Sammy just stood there, waiting. And even with Hercules, the same thing happened. A raised arm, a quick whisper in the ear, and the great savage beast turned tail and strolled straight back to his cage.

The crowd leapt to their feet, clapping and cheering. They had never seen anything like it.

Even the Emperor could not argue with the result – Sammy had beaten the lions, fair and square. He gave Sammy the thumbs up, his life was saved and Sammy was carried from the arena shoulder high.

That night, the Emperor held a feast in Sammy's honour and everyone had a marvellous time.

Dad paused and looked at us both.

"You can't leave it like that," I said. "What did Sammy say to the lions?"

"Well," said Dad, "to each lion, all Sammy said was: 'You know what comes next, don't you? As soon as you've eaten me – the speeches!' "